OXFORD BOOKWORMS LIBRARY
True Stories

Desert, Mountain, Sea

Stage 4 (1400 headwords)

Series Editor: Jennifer Bassett
Founder Editor: Tricia Hedge
Activities Editors: Jennifer Bassett and Alison Baxter

To my family and friends,
for their support

SUE LEATHER

Desert, Mountain, Sea

Retold from

Tracks
by Robyn Davidson

Annapurna: A Woman's Place
by Arlene Blum

At One With The Sea
by Naomi James

OXFORD UNIVERSITY PRESS
2000

Oxford University Press
Great Clarendon Street, Oxford OX2 6DP

Oxford New York
Athens Auckland Bangkok Bogotá Buenos Aires Calcutta Cape Town
Chennai Dar es Salaam Delhi Florence Hong Kong Istanbul Karachi
Kuala Lumpur Madrid Melbourne Mexico City Mumbai Nairobi
Paris São Paulo Singapore Taipei Tokyo Toronto Warsaw
and associated companies in
Berlin Ibadan

OXFORD and OXFORD ENGLISH
are trade marks of Oxford University Press

ISBN 0 19 423031 7

First published in Oxford Bookworms 1989
This second edition published in the Oxford Bookworms Library 2000

The publishers would like to thank
the following for their permission to reproduce photographs:
Dame Naomi James; Arlene Blum and John Cleare/Mountain Camera;
Rick Smolan/Contact/Colorific!

Maps by Vivien McKay
Annapurna diagram by Mike Saunders

Printed in Spain by Unigraf s.l.

CONTENTS

Across the Australian Desert

It was a beautiful Australian morning, sunny and clear. Not far from Alice Springs, in the centre of this huge country, a young woman started on a journey that would take her 2,800 kilometres across the central desert to the western coast of Australia. With her was her dog, Diggity, and four camels. It was the beginning of a very unusual adventure for the young woman, but it was also the end of many months of preparation.

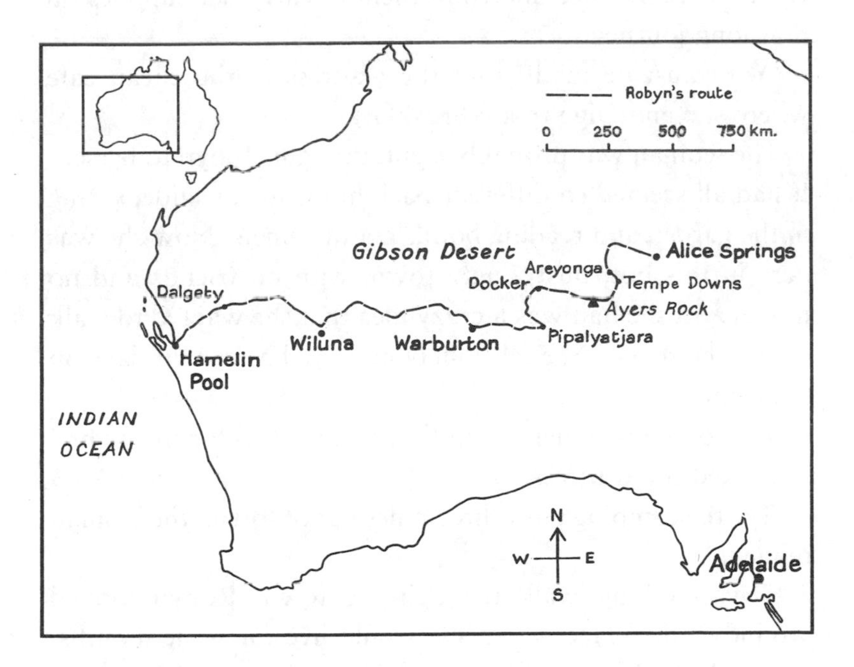

Australia

1

In Alice Springs

Robyn Davidson had first arrived in Alice Springs at five o'clock one morning, over eighteen months ago, with only six dollars in her pocket. She and Diggity had travelled 800 kilometres by train from the city of Adelaide on the southern coast of Australia. Robyn wanted to walk across the central desert of Australia, from Alice Springs to the west coast, with the help of camels. She hoped to find some wild camels here in Alice and train them to carry her supplies on that long journey.

'You must be mad!' said the waitress in the cheap café where she and Diggity ate breakfast.

The woman was probably right, thought Robyn to herself. It had all seemed so different back home in Adelaide, sitting in the garden and reading books about camels. Now she was here in this hot, dusty, ugly town, with no friends and no money. All she had was a crazy idea that she wanted to walk across the desert. She felt lonely and tired after two days on the train.

'Do you know where I can find a cheap bed for the night?' she asked the waitress.

'Try the camping park three miles out of town,' the woman replied.

It was a long walk through the town. Robyn looked around at the place where she would live for some months. About 14,000 people lived in Alice Springs, and 1,000 of them were Aborigines. Most of the white people were government workers, sheep station bosses and lorry drivers. There were also some people who worked in small businesses for the tourists. The town had three pubs, a few hotels and two or three bad restaurants. Alice Springs had a lovely name, but the truth was not at all lovely, thought Robyn.

Robyn slept well that night, and woke up feeling a little happier. Now she had to find a job. Camels were expensive, and she had no money. First, she tried to find work in a pub.

'You can start in two days' time,' said the owner of the first pub she tried. 'You sleep in the back room and all meals are included.' That was perfect. She would have two days to find out about the camel businesses in town.

Camels were first brought into Australia from India and Afghanistan in the 1850s. They carried supplies during the building of the railways. There are now about 10,000 wild camels in Australia. Robyn needed just a few, and she soon learnt that there were three camel farms around Alice Springs. The next day she started her search.

'What do you know about camels?' asked the owner of the first camel farm.

'Not much.'

'And the desert?'

'Not much either but . . .'

'I don't think I can help you, miss.'

This was Sallay Mahomet, the first camel man that Robyn tried. He was a short, strong Afghan with dark eyes. His job was to bring camels from the bush and to sell them as meat to Arab countries. Robyn knew as soon as she saw him that Sallay could teach her a lot about camels, but he was not interested in helping her. Robyn carried on looking.

'I want to train some camels and take them across the desert,' she said to the next camel farmer. This one just laughed at her. Robyn realized that it *did* sound a little crazy. Perhaps she would never find anyone to teach her about camels. The only place left to try was the Posel Farm, owned by a man called Kurt Posel. 'He's a madman,' the townspeople had warned her. It was her last chance.

Kurt Posel was a tall, thin Austrian of about forty-five, who lived at the farm with his small, gentle wife, Gladdy. He kept camels for the tourists, who came to ride on the animals' backs. Almost immediately, he offered Robyn a job for eight months.

'And after that you can buy one of my camels. I'll teach you to train camels and then you can get two wild ones as well. You're very lucky that I'm helping you,' said Kurt, and looked at Robyn with his ice-blue eyes.

Robyn started work at the farm immediately and also kept her job at the pub: She was allowed to have Diggity with her on the farm, and she felt very lucky to have found a job so quickly.

2

The First Step

Robyn woke up at 3.30 every morning. She started work at 4.00, when she went out into the fields to catch the camels. Her job was to bring them in and put saddles on them. The camels spent the day taking the tourists around the farm for a dollar a ride.

Robyn Davidson

As well as this, her main jobs were to keep the yard clean, and to feed the animals. The work was very hard and the hours were long. But in eight months she would have her own camels, and then her adventure could really begin.

In the evenings she carried on working in the pub, and slept in a small room behind it. In a letter to her family she described her new home:

> Only men drink in the pubs here, and most of them drink too much. Often they come into the pub when it opens and they don't leave until closing time, twelve hours later! One of them said to me one night, 'The Aborigines are lazy, they never want to work . . .' I just laughed to myself, because I never see these white men working. They don't like black people. And they don't like women. In fact, they dislike anybody who's different from them.

Robyn did not stay long at the pub. She did not like to hear the mens' talk, and anyway she was much too busy at the farm.

Kurt had eight camels: Biddy, Misch-Misch, Khartoum, Ali, Fahani, Aba, Bubby, and Dookie. They were all different, like human beings, Robyn thought. She liked Dookie most. He was very proud, and she thought he was like a king. She had read many books about camels, but during the next few months she learnt the truth about them. She discovered that they were intelligent (almost as intelligent as Diggity!), playful, patient, hard-working and very interesting. They could also be extremely dangerous. If they became angry, they would kick her or try to sit on her. But she loved them all and loved to watch them hour after hour.

The camels were not a problem, but Kurt was. Robyn soon began to understand why people had warned her about him. He made her work very hard, from early morning until late at night, seven days a week. When she did something wrong, he shouted at her: 'You stupid girl! Never turn your back on a camel!' He stopped her from wearing shoes, so that her feet would become harder, like a camel's. Sometimes, at the end of the day, Robyn's feet were very painful and she could not walk. But the thing that really made Robyn angry was that he was very cruel to the camels and often beat them. She hated to see him treat the animals badly.

The months went by and Robyn learnt something every day. In a strange way, Kurt's unkindness helped her, because it made her strong and fearless. But as she got stronger, Kurt became lazier and lazier, and Robyn had to work harder and harder. Some days, she felt so unhappy that she almost packed her bags and went home. Only Gladdy's kindness stopped her. 'Don't worry, love,' Gladdy used to say. 'It won't be long now.'

One day, towards the end of the eight months, Kurt came out to talk to Robyn as she was cleaning the yard.

'Tomorrow you must get up two hours earlier to bring the camels in,' he said.

Robyn felt so tired that she suddenly became very angry. 'How can you ask me to do that?' she asked. 'You're lazy. You make me do your work as well as mine!'

Kurt looked at Robyn and shouted back: 'Then you must leave!'

The next morning, Robyn packed her bags and left the farm. She felt very miserable. Now she would never get her camels. This was the end of her adventure. She knew that Kurt had made her leave the farm so that he would not have to give her the camels. He was mean, as well as lazy and cruel.

Just when Robyn was feeling that she would have to go back to Adelaide, Sallay Mahomet came back into her life. He had heard about Robyn's problems at the Posel farm, and he felt very sorry for her. 'Come and work for me for two months and I'll give you two of my wild camels,' he told her. Robyn almost kissed the old gentleman, but she decided to kiss Diggity instead. She was in business again.

During the next two months, Sallay taught her a lot about camels. She learnt how to repair saddles, how to use ropes, how to tie up a camel and many other things. Everything Robyn learnt would be extremely useful to her when she was alone in the bush. Sallay was much kinder than Kurt, too.

The day finally arrived when Sallay gave her the two camels he had promised. They were Alcoota Kate, an older, very strong camel, and Zeleika, a beautiful young one. She would have to train them, but now at last she had her own camels. As she led them off Sallay's farm one lovely Australian morning, Robyn felt very happy and very proud.

3

Camel Time

Robyn went to live on a nearby farm, called Basso's Farm, with her camels – 'her girls' – and Diggity. Her plan now was to train the camels and to start her trip as soon as she could. But she still had problems.

'She's got a bad chest. You'll have to give her injections every day.' The doctor did not sound very hopeful. Robyn had asked him to come to look at Alcoota Kate, who was getting thinner and thinner and seemed to be very ill.

'Will she be all right?' Robyn asked.

'I'm not sure . . . she's very old,' the young man replied.

Kate had been used for carrying supplies some years before. She had been treated very badly and as a result she hated humans. It was therefore very difficult to get near enough to her to give her the injections she needed. Robyn tried as hard as she could.

Zeleika was thin too, but with good, regular food she seemed to get better. Zelly was a very gentle animal, and not as afraid of humans as Kate. She loved to kick though, like most camels, and Robyn was careful when she was near her. She wanted to ride Zelly, and use Kate to carry supplies.

Robyn's nearest neighbour at the farm was an Aborigine woman, Ada Baxter. She was a friendly, older woman who always called Robyn 'my daughter'. Although she had been treated badly by the white people, she did not seem to have any bad feeling towards them. She and Robyn became good friends. Robyn looked forward to meeting more Aborigines when she was travelling in the bush. She wanted to learn about them.

One day, after Robyn had been at Basso's Farm for a month, Sallay came to visit her and to have a look at the camels, who were playing in the yard.

'Zeleika is going to have a baby!' he suddenly said.

Robyn had not noticed this at all, but she believed Sallay, because he knew so much about camels. 'My God, what can I do if she has the baby on the trip?' she asked.

'Don't worry. Just tie the baby up and put it on the mother's back until it's strong enough to walk,' said Sallay. 'It won't be a problem.'

Kate, however, was becoming a real problem. She was getting sicker and sicker, and nothing seemed to help. She got so many illnesses that Robyn finally decided that she was just too old. Sallay's advice was to destroy her – to shoot her. Robyn had never killed anything before, and to kill a camel . . . to kill an animal she loved . . . she did not want to think about it. In the end, though, the camel was too ill, too much in pain. Robyn knew that she would have to do it.

When she had shot the animal through the head, Robyn cried for hours. She cried for Kate and she cried for herself.

She had spent the last eighteen months here for nothing. She still only had one camel and her dream of crossing the desert seemed further away than ever before.

As usual when things looked very bad, Robyn had some good luck. Kurt Posel had sold his farm to a man who did not know how to look after camels. This man sold Robyn two bull camels, Bub and Dookie the king, for 700 dollars. She did not have the money, of course, but she was able to borrow it. Bull camels were not the best, because they were very strong and could be violent. 'But at least,' thought Robyn to herself, 'I've got three camels now.'

Zeleika, Bub and Dookie soon became very good friends. They often went into the bush together, and sometimes it took Robyn a long time to find them. One morning, she woke up and went out into the yard as usual to see them but could not find them anywhere. They had disappeared. After searching for an hour, Robyn and Diggity found the camels' tracks, going east. They walked and walked. Finally, Diggity became too tired to walk any longer, so Robyn left her under a tree and told her to wait. Diggity did not want to wait, but she obeyed Robyn.

It was late that night when Robyn returned. Diggity, worried and thirsty, was still waiting under the tree, and did a little dance of happiness when she saw Robyn. The camels, however, were still missing.

The next day Zeleika, Bub, and Dookie had still not appeared, and some kind people from the town offered to take Robyn to look for them in their small aeroplane. Robyn was very worried. She promised herself that if she found the camels she would start her trip immediately. They flew around all day, and Robyn thought she saw the camels many times, but each time it was horses or some other animal.

Finally, as the pilot turned the plane to go back, Robyn looked round for the last time. Suddenly she saw them. Yes, it was them – the gentle Zeleika, Bub, and Dookie the king. Robyn could not believe her luck. 'I'm going to start this adventure now!' she said out loud.

4

The Journey Begins

Water – four big containers just for the camels, clothes, ropes, radio, cassette recorder with tapes of the Aboriginal language Pitjantjara, maps, compass, rifle, knife – these were just a few of the supplies that the camels had to carry. Then of course there was the food: bags full of oranges, potatoes, rice, tea, sugar, . . . Every day it took Robyn two hours to prepare the camels for the day's walk.

On her first night under the desert sky, Robyn had two big worries: first, losing the camels, and second, scorpions, which are small insects with a painful and dangerous bite. Fortunately, when she woke up next morning, the camels were still there and she had not been bitten by a scorpion. In fact, the main danger was from wild bull camels. 'Shoot first, and ask questions later!' Sallay had told her. This was why Robyn carried the rifle, though she hoped she would never have to use it.

It was a strange group that walked off into the desert. First came Robyn riding Bub, then came Zelly and Dookie, and finally, some metres behind, Zelly's new baby, Goliath. Diggity could be anywhere, as she usually liked to run around looking for wild rabbits. Sometimes they were lucky enough to catch a rabbit for dinner. If not, Robyn ate rice and vegetables.

She was planning to walk about thirty-two kilometres a day, six days a week, for between six and eight months, so the food she ate was very important. She had learnt about wild plants from her Aboriginal friends in Alice Springs. She knew which ones were good to eat, and as a result she became very healthy and strong.

In the evenings when the camels were unpacked, and the

Robyn, Diggity, and the camels begin their long journey.

day's work was finished, Robyn listened to her tapes and tried to teach herself Pitjantjara. It was not easy, but she was an enthusiastic student, and hoped to speak a little of the language when she arrived in the village of Areyonga.

Areyonga was an Aboriginal village with only about ten white people. A few kilometres outside the village Robyn was met by children talking excitedly to her in Pitjantjara. When she arrived in the village, everyone came out to say hello to her, because they all thought that the *kungka ramarama* (crazy woman) could speak their language very well. This was not really true, but Robyn enjoyed trying to use the few words she knew.

Robyn stayed in Areyonga for three days with the village schoolteacher and his family. She noticed that a lot of the old Aborigines were blind, and she asked the schoolteacher about it.

'It's trachoma – a serious disease of the eye. It's one of the many illnesses the Australian Aborigines have,' he said.

'What causes it?' asked Robyn.

'Oh, bad housing, poor medical care and bad food – all caused by our government, unfortunately.'

After their rest, Robyn and the animals went on to the Tempe Downs sheep station, about sixty kilometres away. Now the countryside became wilder and wilder, more like the desert, and Robyn began to see the tracks of wild camels on the ground. After Tempe Downs, where they collected fresh water, they went on to Ayers Rock.

Ayers Rock is a huge red rock, which rises up out of the desert sand. Robyn thought it was the most beautiful thing she had ever seen. For the Aborigines, it has a special meaning and Robyn could understand why. She camped near it, and tried to avoid the many tourists who visit it.

When she opened her eyes the next morning, she could not believe what she saw. Wild bull camels were running towards her! She quickly felt for her rifle and fired ('Shoot first, and ask questions later'). Soon there was blood everywhere; one camel was dead and the others had run off into the desert. Dookie looked afraid. Robyn was shaking with fear and anger. Shooting the wild camel had made her think of Kate again and there were tears in her eyes.

Ayers Rock is a huge red rock, which rises up out of the desert sand.

5

Mr Eddie

A few days later, Robyn and her companions arrived in the small town of Docker. Now she was in the middle of Aborigine country. The countryside was full of places, like Ayers Rock, which were special to the Aborigines. Robyn planned to go from Docker to Pipalyatjara, but she wanted to avoid the usual routes and go across the country.

'You need an old Aborigine man to go with you,' someone told her in Docker. 'Women aren't allowed to go to some of these places. You should have a guide.'

Robyn knew that this was true, so she asked the old men in the town if one of them would go with her to Pipalyatjara. They were all very polite, but the answer was 'no'. Robyn did not look forward to travelling the 250 kilometres alone, but a few days later she left Docker for Pipalyatjara.

One night, about forty kilometres from Docker, Robyn was sitting at her camp fire with Diggity when she heard the sound of a car in the distance. 'Who do you think it is, Diggity?' Diggity immediately jumped up and started barking, as she usually did when she heard a noise.

It was Aborigines – one young man and three old ones. They stayed the night and gave some of their rabbit supper to Robyn. One of the old men spoke good English and he talked and talked. Robyn liked one of the others very much. He was very small and thin and quiet. He did not speak much English, so Robyn spoke to him with her few words of Pitjantjara.

Early next morning, the men decided that one of them should go with Robyn to Pipalyatjara. She was delighted when she heard that it was going to be the small, quiet one. 'Mr Eddie,' said the man and pointed to himself. Robyn smiled at the little man. She knew that they were going to be good friends.

At first, Robyn was worried that Mr Eddie would not be able to walk thirty-two kilometres a day. He was old, and did not look very strong. In fact, he could easily walk eighty kilometres a day. Robyn also found that she no longer needed maps. Mr Eddie knew exactly where he was going. They spoke to each other in Pitjantjara. Sometimes it was difficult, but they always found something to laugh about together. They liked to laugh at the tourists with their cameras. They became good friends on the journey, and Eddie fell in love with Robyn's rifle, which he kept near to him day and night.

Two days later they arrived in Pipalyatjara, Eddie's home. Robyn knew Glendle, an official there, and she stayed with him for a few days. He told her about the work he was doing with the Aborigines.

'We have to help the Aborigines to fight for their land,' said Glendle at supper one evening. 'But the problem is that they don't think that the land really belongs to them.'

Robyn did not understand. 'What do you mean?' she asked.

'Well, for them the idea of owning land is strange – the land can own *them*, but they can't own the land.'

Robyn learnt a lot about the Aborigines in Pipalyatjara. Soon, however, it was time to go again. It was now June, and she had only completed a third of her journey. She still had

Mr Eddie and Robyn became good friends on the journey.

the Gibson Desert ahead of her, and she wanted to get across it before the hotter weather in late September.

She asked Eddie if he would go with her to Warburton, a town 320 kilometres to the west. At first he said no, because he was 'too old', and anyway he needed new shoes. But Robyn promised to buy him some new shoes and his own rifle when they arrived in Warburton. Finally, the old man agreed, and they left.

That evening, Eddie took Robyn away from the route she had planned, because he had been born in this country and knew it very well. For a week they walked through the country, and, when they camped at night, Eddie told her many stories about the Aborigines and their customs.

They were almost at Warburton, but how much further

was it exactly? Robyn asked some young Aborigines in a car. 'Little bit long way, maybe two sleeps,' they replied. It was always like this when she asked an Aborigine about distances. When she told them she was going to the sea (*uru pulka* – big lake), they said, 'Long, long way, too many sleeps that uru pulka.'

On their last night together, Eddie told Robyn that he would find her another guide after Warburton. Robyn asked him not to do this. The next part would be 640 kilometres of waterless desert – the Gibson Desert – and Robyn had decided that she wanted to go across it alone. Eddie shook his head sadly, but Robyn had made her decision.

Glendle had driven from Pipalyatjara to take Eddie home. Before Eddie left, Robyn gave him his new rifle. Eddie took it

Robyn was happy to be alone again in the desert.

proudly, smiled at her, held her arm and shook his head. Then he got into Glendle's car and they drove off. Robyn was alone once more.

6

To the Sea

Robyn wrote in her diary:

> The country is dry and hot, although it is still only spring. At night and in the early morning it is quite cool, but by midday it is boiling hot again. The walking's difficult too; there's nothing but spinifex (a kind of tough, sharp grass) and sandhills. The poor camels can't find very much to eat, and are becoming thinner and thinner. Zeleika, who is feeding her baby, little Goliath, looks terribly thin. I must get to the sea before the summer starts.

Robyn had loved travelling with Eddie, but now she was happy to be alone again in the desert. She did not feel lonely because Diggity was with her. In her diary she wrote that Diggity 'is as good as a human friend, and she's a great listener'. They had a special friendship.

At Wiluna, the first real town since Alice Springs, Robyn got a muzzle for Diggity to wear round her mouth. The local farmers put poison on the ground to kill the dingos, which are Australian wild dogs. The farmers do not like dingos because they kill sheep. Robyn was afraid that her dog would eat the poison. But Diggity hated her muzzle, and looked very miserable when Robyn made her wear it. In the end, Robyn took it off, and hoped that Diggity would not go near the poison.

One night, when Robyn was resting, Diggity started running about in a strange way. 'What's the matter, Diggity? Where've you been?' said Robyn.

The dog ran backwards and forwards. She was clearly in pain. Then she came and put her head between Robyn's legs. 'You can't be poisoned, you're my dog and you can't die,' Robyn said.

Then she remembered reading what to do in case of strychnine poisoning: 'Swing the animal around your head, in order to drive the poison out of the body.' She picked up the frightened Diggity, and began to swing her round and round her head. But she knew there was almost no chance that her dog would live. Diggity escaped from Robyn, and ran away. She was barking like a mad dog. Robyn followed her with her gun. Diggity was now in a lot of pain, and Robyn knew what she had to do. After she had killed the dog, she ran away and was violently sick.

The next morning, Robyn packed up and left the place where Diggity, her best friend, had died. She knew that she had to carry on walking.

That day, Robyn walked over fifty kilometres. Without Diggity she walked much faster. She missed her little friend very badly, and she wanted to finish the journey as quickly as possible. She now took only half an hour – not two hours – to get the camels ready every morning.

Robyn was thin, but very healthy and very brown. She usually wore very few clothes, and had not washed herself well for weeks. She felt that she looked rather strange. 'If my friends could see me now,' she told herself, 'they would think I was completely mad.'

With only 300 kilometres to go, the final disaster happened. Zeleika started bleeding very badly. She was extremely thin and Robyn was sure she would die. There was nothing to eat, and it was getting hotter every day. Robyn gave Zelly forty pills a day, hidden inside an orange. Would she be all right until they reached Dalgety, where there was a farm? Until then, Robyn tried to keep little Goliath away from his sick mother.

At Dalgety Farm, Margot and David Steadman gave poor Zelly some good food to eat. With their care the sick camel got much better. After a week at the farm Zelly had stopped bleeding and was getting a little fatter. Robyn was sure that Zelly could now manage to walk to the coast.

After so much desert, it was wonderful to be near the sea.

After their rest at Dalgety, Robyn and the camels walked on to the sea, about 200 kilometres away. It was the end of their journey. Robyn wanted to show her camels the Indian Ocean, the *uru pulka* of the Aborigines. The camels had never seen so much water before, and they became very excited. Goliath, who was still very young, ran straight into the sea for a swim; the others just ran playfully along the beach. After so much desert, it was wonderful to be near the sea. Robyn and her camels spent a week at Hamelin Pool, just resting.

Now, for the first time since she had started the journey, Robyn really thought about the future. She planned to leave the camels with some friends, Jan and David, who lived on a farm at Woodleigh, not far away. Jan and David loved camels almost as much as Robyn did, and she knew that Dookie, Bub, Zeleika, and of course Goliath, would have a good home there. But what about Robyn? For the moment, she did not know where to go or what to do. She would miss her camels and she would miss this wonderful journey. It had ended too quickly.

Robyn looked at the ocean. It was difficult to believe that she really had walked 2,800 kilometres across the desert. She thought about the people she had met who had helped her – Sallay, Gladdy, Glendle, and dear Mr Eddie. And Kurt too, in a strange kind of way. She thought sadly of Diggity, and proudly of her camels, who had survived that long, long journey. Finally, she thought about herself. She had done it, her dream had come true. She knew that wherever she went, whatever she did, her life would never be the same again.

Climbing Annapurna

It was 8.30 a.m. on August 6th 1978. After a journey of twenty-four hours, an aeroplane landed at Kathmandu airport in Nepal. On the plane was a group of eleven women. They were all very excited but also a little afraid, as they had flown from America to climb one of the highest, most dangerous mountains in the world. The name of the mountain was Annapurna.

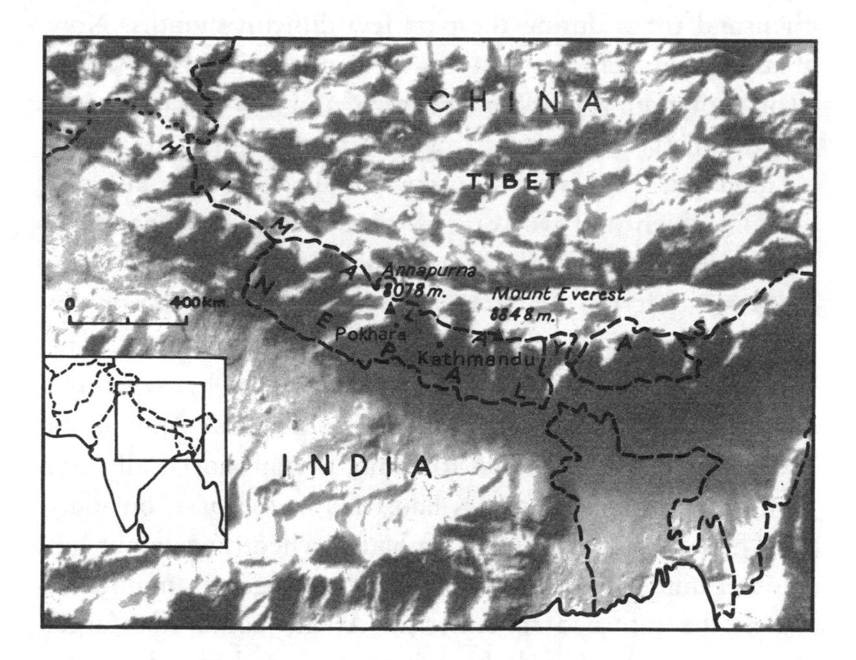

Nepal and the Himalayas

1

Climbers Wanted

The leader of the group was Arlene Blum, an American mountaineer with many years experience of climbing high mountains. For her, this day was the result of two years of planning. She smiled as she walked down the steps of the plane and saw the Nepalese newspapermen running up to her.

'Why do you want to climb Annapurna? Why all women?' they asked her.

These were the same questions Arlene had asked herself a thousand times during the past few difficult months. Now that she was here the answers seemed simpler than before. 'This mountain is 8,000 metres high, and if we succeed we'll be the first Americans and the first women to climb Annapurna. And why all women? Because we all love climbing high and we want to give women the chance to climb one of the world's highest mountains.'

As she left the plane and walked towards the airport buildings, Arlene remembered how it had all started. The idea of climbing Annapurna had first come to her when she was in the Himalayas in 1976. The beautiful Annapurna seemed a perfect mountain to climb, though not at all easy. Thirteen groups of climbers had tried in the past, but only four had succeeded. Eight men had reached the summit but another nine had lost their lives on the dangerous mountain. When she returned to America, Arlene could not forget Annapurna. She talked about it to two good friends in San Francisco, Vera Watson and Irene Miller.

Vera Watson was forty-six and a computer scientist. She had been climbing high mountains for many years. She did not look tough, but she was a woman with a very strong character. She had climbed Aconcagua in Argentina alone, and she had always wanted to climb in the Himalayas. Irene Miller was also a scientist, and the mother of two daughters. She knew that the expedition was dangerous and that she could be killed; but she also knew that, at forty-two, she would probably not get another chance to climb to 8,000 metres. Both Vera and Irene were enthusiastic about Arlene's idea.

Their first job was to choose the other members of the team. They needed women who were strong – physically *and* mentally; women who would not stop when they became very cold, very hungry, or very tired. They needed a doctor to take care of the mountaineers if they became ill or were hurt high on the mountain. They also needed someone to make a film of the climb, so that the world could learn about it later. Most important of all, they needed women who had climbed high mountains before. They put an advertisement in a climbing magazine:

WOMEN CLIMBERS WANTED

Would you like to join an all-women's expedition to Annapurna? You must be an experienced high-altitude climber, strong, enthusiastic and a hard worker! If you think this is for YOU, please contact:

Arlene Blum, Berkeley, California, USA

Many women wrote to them from all over the world, but

The Annapurna team. (Arlene Blum is standing on the right)

they could choose only ten. When the final team was chosen, the youngest was twenty years old, the oldest was fifty.

For Arlene, finding the climbers was only the first step. The team needed another important thing: money. There were long talks at Vera Watson's house, when they discussed how to make the 80,000 dollars they would need for the expedition. With the help of enthusiastic friends, they organized dances, sports, and parties. They even sold expedition T-shirts. After many months, and a lot of hard work, they finally had the money they needed.

Now at last they were in Kathmandu, the city where their great adventure would begin. Arlene looked round at the women in the airport. They looked tired after the long journey from San Francisco, but happy to be in Nepal at last. There had been so many friends and families at the airport to say goodbye. It had been difficult to leave the people they loved. Irene had looked so sad when she said goodbye to her daughters. Arlene too had found it very difficult to leave her boyfriend, John. For all of them there was the chance that they would never see their families or friends again.

All climbing in the Himalayas is dangerous. One in ten of the people who go there do not come back. Annapurna was very dangerous because of its avalanches. Arlene knew the dangers of avalanches very well. On the expedition film she said:

'Until a few years ago I thought that mountains were the happiest places in the world. I thought that only good things happened on mountains. Then a very good friend of mine, John Henry Hall, was killed in an avalanche on Mount St Elias in Canada. Since then I have really understood the dangers. With avalanches there's nothing you can do . . .'

It was difficult for Arlene to think about avalanches, but she knew that, as the team leader, she had to accept the dangers. Now, as she led the women into the airport buildings, she tried to forget her own fears. She was the leader of the expedition, and it was her job to get these women to the top of Annapurna safely. She felt responsible for them all.

2

Kathmandu

As the group arrived at the modern Siddhartha Hotel, Joan Firey and Alison Chadwick, two other members of the team, welcomed them enthusiastically. These women were two of the most experienced women mountaineers in the world. Joan, at forty-nine, had climbed mountains all over America and Canada, and was very confident that this team would succeed. Alison was a British climber who had climbed higher than any of them. They had been in Kathmandu for a week buying food and getting everything ready. Now they waved and smiled as the others arrived. They were soon excitedly telling their friends about all the plans they had made.

For the next few days, the women enjoyed the sights, sounds, and smells of Kathmandu. Everything was so different from home. The streets were full of animals, people selling food, women dressed in colourful clothes, and the sound of Nepalese music. Arlene loved it here, though, as leader of the expedition, she had a lot to do. One of her jobs was to meet the Sherpas they had hired to carry loads on the mountain.

The Sherpas live in eastern Nepal. Their villages are high up in the mountains, often over 3,500 metres high. They know the mountains very well and are excellent climbers and porters. Some climbing teams use Sherpas, others don't, but Arlene thought that their help would make the climb easier and safer.

Alison Chadwick, however, disagreed with Arlene. 'Why are we using Sherpas?' she asked Arlene. 'We should climb Annapurna without men.'

Arlene was silent. She knew that they would need the Sherpas if conditions on the mountain became difficult. She wanted the climb to be as safe as possible. She listened to Alison's opinion, but Arlene knew that *she*, as leader, had to decide in the end.

Another problem for Arlene was food. She had a meeting with Joan, who was taking care of food for the expedition. 'How's the shopping, Joan?' she asked her. Joan gave her a list of everything she had bought. 'I don't think there are enough different kinds of food,' said Arlene. 'We can't eat only rice. People will stop eating on the mountain if the food isn't interesting. We need more meat and fruit.'

'It's too late now,' said Joan.

Arlene almost became angry, because they had talked about this same problem before. She had seen climbers who had stopped eating high on the mountain, and she did not want to see this expedition fail for the same reasons. 'Buy the food today, Joan,' she ordered. 'It's very important.'

Arlene also had worries of a different kind. Annie Whitehouse, who was twenty-one, was falling in love with Yeshi, the Nepalese cook. One day when they returned from a shopping trip, Annie said to Arlene, 'When I met him, I felt that I had known him for years!'

Arlene looked at Annie's happy, smiling face. 'Remember the rules of the expedition – no falling in love!' Arlene warned her. Annie just laughed.

The next day the expedition left Kathmandu for Pokhara,

where the long walk to the mountain would start. It was 130 kilometres to the base of the mountain, and it would take them eleven days to get there. Once they had left Pokhara and were walking through the beautiful Nepalese countryside, the problems seemed to disappear for a while. The countryside was so green, and there were so many new types of trees and flowers. Vera Karmakova, who was very interested in plants, collected many of the unusual flowers. The women enjoyed the easy walking and the stops at the villages along the way. Piro Kramar, the team doctor, and Annie Whitehouse, who was a nurse, gave advice and medicines to the people in each village. The expedition was very popular with the people of the countryside.

Then the monsoon rains came. August was the worst month for rain. Near the village of Ghorapani it suddenly started to rain very hard. The rain brought new problems for Arlene. Lopsang Tsering, the 'sirdar', or head Sherpa, came to speak to her. He always called her 'Bara Memsahib', which means 'Woman Leader' in Nepalese.

'Bara Memsahib,' he said. 'Five porters have returned to Pokhara – very bad rain.'

Arlene knew that on some expeditions all the porters just ran away in bad weather, and left the climbers with no one to carry their equipment. She hoped that this would not happen on their Annapurna climb.

Lopsang could see that Arlene was worried, and said, 'Cheer up, Bara Memsahib. I will talk to them.' Lopsang always tried to help Arlene and often worked fourteen hours a day to make the expedition successful.

Annie and Alison had gone ahead to establish Base Camp,

at almost 4,500 metres. When the other women arrived at the camp, they saw a stone with the names of the seven climbers who had died on this side of the mountain. Arlene looked at the stone. Once again, she was reminded of the dangers of this adventure. Now, the low-altitude porters left their loads and returned to Pokhara. Only the Sherpas and the women were left with the beautiful, dangerous Annapurna, which looked down on them from thousands of metres above.

3

Base Camp

Suddenly a very loud noise made Arlene jump. It was the noise of an avalanche coming down from near the summit of Annapurna. It was before breakfast on the second morning at Base Camp, and Arlene had walked a little way up towards the mountain. Now she was sitting looking down at the tents below. She needed to be alone to think about the climb. She wanted to plan how to get to the top of this mountain. When she heard the avalanche, she again remembered her friend who had died, and she felt very afraid.

On most mountains, avalanches are unusual very early in the morning. On Annapurna, avalanches could happen at any time of the night or day. It was almost impossible to avoid them. Arlene knew that, if they were caught by an avalanche, someone could be killed. Fortunately, this avalanche was too far away from Base Camp to worry the climbers. But perhaps they would not always be so lucky.

Arlene now had to put these worries out of her head,

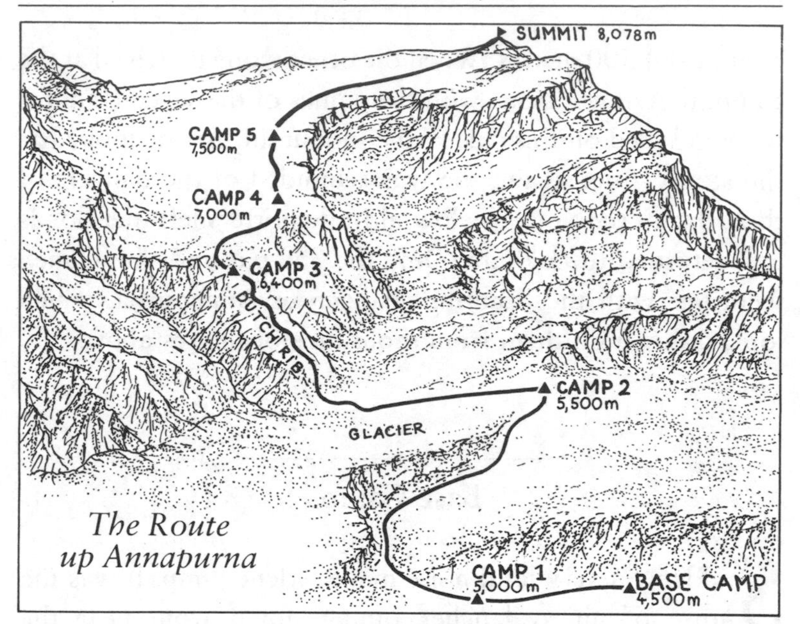

The Route up Annapurna

because the really serious work of climbing the mountain was just beginning. Tomorrow Alison Chadwick and Liz Klobusicky would go up to over 5,000 metres to make Camp 1. In the end, there would be five camps at different points on the mountain. Each camp would have a tent and some food. The women would walk between the camps in small teams of two or three, carrying food and equipment. The 'summit team' of two or three women would start from Camp 5. This was the safest way of climbing Annapurna. If there was a storm and conditions became too difficult, climbers could come down to a lower camp to find tents and food.

'Bara Memsahib,' said Lopsang, when Arlene returned to the camp. 'You must not sleep at Camp 2 before the middle of September. We should offer food and drink to the mountain gods before you begin climbing the most dangerous part of the mountain above Camp 2. The middle of September is the best time to go higher.'

Arlene knew that the monsoon rains would finish in the middle of September, and so it was a good idea to wait. For the next two weeks they could carry food and equipment up the mountain to prepare for this dangerous climb above Camp 2. Lopsang helped Arlene to plan the climb carefully. They had to reach the summit during a break between the monsoons and the really bad winter weather, when climbing high would become impossible.

Next day there was fine weather and the walking conditions were good. Liz and Alison were happy to be climbing the mountain at last, and they left Base Camp early to try to establish Camp 1 on the mountain. Before they went, they spoke to the women who were making the film.

Liz, a young American climber who worked as a school-teacher in Germany, said: 'This is a great opportunity for women mountaineers.'

'The really difficult part has not yet begun,' said Alison. 'We will need to be both brave and strong as we go higher up this mountain.'

It seemed a long, long wait for the others at Base Camp below. Finally, after some hours, they heard a voice coming from the radio. It was Liz Klobusicky. 'This is Liz and Alison at Camp 1. Repeat, we are at Camp 1. It took us four and a half hours, and the walk is not too difficult. The Camp was established at 2.30 p.m. on August 28th.' Everyone at Base Camp cheered. The first step on the mountain had been taken.

4

Storms and Other Problems

On September 3rd, Arlene wrote in her diary:

> At last we seem to be working together as a team, and everyone seems happier. It must be the hard work of carrying loads between Camp 1 and Camp 2. It will take us two weeks to carry enough tents and equipment to Camp 2 before our climbers go on up the mountain. We must be careful climbing between Camps 1 and 2. We have to cross the glacier and at any moment we could fall down a crevasse and be lost forever! We also have to worry about the effects of thin air at high altitudes. Camp 2 is at over 5,500 metres, and there is not much oxygen in the air. We have found that it's best to climb only 350 metres a day. We work for two days and rest for one. At this altitude, people often have headaches, and sleep badly. They can't think clearly, and they don't want to eat – even chocolate doesn't taste good.

But the team was certainly happier now that the hard work had begun. At nights they sat together in the tents and sang songs after dinner. Arlene was beginning to feel that her job as leader was not so difficult after all. But time was passing and she had to start thinking about the best way to reach the summit, and who should go. On big Himalayan expeditions like this, only two or three climbers could hope to reach the summit. All the other members of the expedition helped by carrying equipment and food up the mountain. This work was very important, but Arlene knew that all the women really wanted to be summit climbers.

Which women would climb the next, and most dangerous, part of the mountain first? The climb from Camp 2 to Camp 3, at 6,400 metres, was the most difficult part of the mountain. It was called 'The Dutch Rib' because it was the route the Dutch team had taken on their expedition in 1977. The route was extremely narrow – often only a few centimetres wide – with drops of hundreds of metres on each side. Although it was the most difficult way up, it was safer than the routes taken by the French and British expeditions because there was not so much danger from avalanches.

'Only the four most experienced ice climbers should lead the next climb, from Camp 2 to Camp 3,' said Arlene to the team as they were sitting at breakfast some days later. 'Liz and Alison will lead the first day, Vera Karmakova and Piro the next. The rest of us will continue carrying between Camps 1 and 2.'

The leading climbers would fix ropes so that the other climbers could climb the difficult places more easily. As Arlene had thought, some of the other women were disappointed.

'Everyone should get a chance to lead,' said Vera Watson.

Others agreed with Vera, but Margi Rusmore, one of the youngest members, finally said: 'I think Arlene's plan is good. We should try it. If it doesn't work, we can change it.'

Things went well for a while, but on September 18th Irene's voice came onto the radio from Camp 2. 'There's half a metre of new snow here, and the wind is terrible!'

At Base Camp, Arlene immediately became worried, and was afraid that an avalanche would follow. She was right. 'Come back down. It could last for days,' warned Arlene, though she knew that coming down would also be dangerous. At Base Camp below, the others waited for hours and hours. Finally Alison, Irene and Piro appeared through the snow and wind. They were exhausted, wet and disappointed – but safe.

The storm continued the next day, and Arlene ordered a rest day. Anyway, it was impossible to climb in this wind and snow. Their clothes and equipment were very wet, and it was very difficult to get dry again. The women and Sherpas spent the day talking and resting, though the storm was still bad, and they could hear avalanches across the valley. Yeshi, the cook, was reminded of the 1974 French expedition to Mount Everest on which he had climbed. An avalanche had killed six people; the leader of the team and five Sherpas had died, all friends of his. 'I'll never climb again,' said Yeshi. This was why he had become a cook. It was much safer.

Next day, the hard work of carrying loads between Camps 1, 2 and now 3 continued. By now, Arlene had made the trip from Camp 1 to Camp 2 five times. The journey from Camp 2 to Camp 3 was extremely dangerous with a heavy load. It would be very easy to fall off the Dutch Rib. They were above 6,000 metres there, and there was so little oxygen that the climbers had to breathe several times for each step they took.

There were also the avalanches which came down the mountain night and day. On the night of September 25th, Arlene was woken at two o'clock in the morning by the frightening sound of an avalanche. There were also very

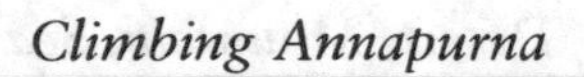

It was hard work carrying loads between the camps.

strong winds and the tents were shaking. After that, Arlene did not sleep at all. 'Why did I choose Annapurna?' she asked herself again and again. 'It's more dangerous than any other mountain – even Everest.'

It was becoming more and more dangerous to continue up the mountain. Irene had decided not to go higher than Camp 2. 'My daughter Teresa is still only thirteen. She needs a mother, and I don't want to die. It's too dangerous to go higher now,' she told Arlene. All the women were worried about the avalanche danger. It sometimes seemed crazy to go on.

Then something happened which made them stop thinking about avalanches for a while. On September 28th, five angry Sherpas left Camp 2. Only Yeshi, who was still very friendly with Annie, remained.

'We are going back to Kathmandu,' the Sherpas told Arlene.

Arlene was extremely worried about the dangers of climbing without them.

'Let them go,' said Alison, who had never wanted the Sherpas on the climb. 'It will be better without them.'

But Arlene knew that the climb would take much longer without the Sherpas, who helped to carry food and equipment between the camps. So early next morning, Arlene and Vera Karmakova went down to Base Camp to talk to the angry Sherpas, and to find out why they had gone.

Arlene was happy to see Lopsang as they arrived at Base Camp. 'The Sherpas want more money and better equipment,' he said.

Arlene was glad that it was not a more serious problem,

though she did not think the Sherpas had behaved well. 'The Sherpas already have very good equipment and pay. They were wrong to leave us,' she told Lopsang, 'but we'll give them 1293 rupees each – nearly forty days' pay. They must go back up to Camp 2 immediately!'

Something else seemed to be worrying Lopsang. 'You should have men on the first summit team. We don't want you women to disappear on the mountain!'

Arlene smiled to herself, and said, 'No. This is a women's expedition. The first summit team is women only; the second team can have Sherpas.'

The next afternoon, the Sherpas were paid and soon they were working again.

5

The Summit

'Who will be in the summit teams?' It was Annie who asked the question, but Arlene knew that all the women were wondering the same thing. Only three women would get the chance to be in the first attempt to reach the summit. They would be the strongest, most experienced members of the expedition. Most important of all, they would be the women who were still very healthy after more than a month on the mountain. There would be a second team of three more women, but perhaps they would not get a chance to try for the summit. The weather could become very bad . . . or a disaster could happen on the first attempt. Also, their supplies of oxygen were not very big.

It was now October 8th. Irene and Piro had reached Camp 4, at over 7,000 metres and soon the bad winter weather would start. They had to try for the summit soon. It was not an easy job for Arlene to choose the right team. As she explained later: 'On expeditions like this, people usually get weaker and weaker. Finally, only one or two climbers are strong enough to reach the top. But after forty days on Annapurna, most of the climbers were still strong enough to try. Only Joan (who was ill), Liz (who had returned to Germany), and myself were not hoping to reach the summit.' Arlene had decided some time ago that she did not want to climb to the top of Annapurna. She just wanted to do her job as leader.

Finally, on October 8th, Arlene told the others her plan. 'The first summit team will be Irene, Vera Karmakova, and Piro. They will use oxygen. Two Sherpas will stay at Camp 5, in case they are needed. The women must try to reach the summit between 14th and 16th October. The second team, following the next day, will be Vera Watson, Alison, and Annie, with two Sherpas.'

The next day, the first team went up to Camp 4 to prepare for the summit. Irene explained the plan to Vera Karmakova and Piro: 'Camp 5 is at 7,500 metres – there is only half as much oxygen as at sea level. The longer we stay there, the weaker we'll become. Also, the cold and wind will be extreme. We should stay there only one night, then try for the summit the next day.'

Down below, at Camps 3 and 4, conditions were not much better. Margi's feet had frozen with the cold. At Camp 3, Arlene put a bottle of hot water in her sleeping bag for the night and by morning the water was ice. There was also their old friend, the avalanche. Lopsang called Arlene on the radio from Base Camp: 'Avalanches are very bad this year all over Nepal. Most expeditions will not succeed. After two climbers have reached the top, we should go home.' The news from Kathmandu was that five climbing expeditions in the Himalayas had already decided to return home.

Climbers at each of the camps on Annapurna could now only look upwards to the icy summit – and wait. The morning of October 15th was fine and calm, and from Base Camp they saw four climbers leaving Camp 5 early in the morning. They were Irene Miller, Vera Karmakova, and two Sherpas. 'What's happened to Piro?' they wondered. They would not know the answer to this question until some time later.

Down at Camp 3, the second team were waiting for their chance to try for the summit. Vera Watson and Alison were still very enthusiastic, but Annie was not sure that she wanted to go to the top. 'There may be no oxygen – it's too dangerous,' she told Arlene.

Arlene understood Annie's fears, and warned Vera and Alison of the dangers again and again.

'Don't worry so much,' said Alison. 'We'll be fine.'

Irene and Vera Karmakova, in the first summit team, could only carry enough oxygen for six hours. They therefore had to get as high as possible without using it. From Base Camp, which had the best view, members of the team watched the summit climbers. Up above, Irene and Vera were breathing six times for each step, and after two and a half hours, they started to use oxygen.

Annapurna – a beautiful, dangerous mountain

Down at Base Camp, the film makers were busy writing about the moment they had all waited for:

> Hour follows hour, with the rest of the team watching and waiting down below. Each step is slow and painful. It is only just over 700 metres from Camp 5 to the summit, but it takes them eight hours. At 3.30 p.m. on October 15th 1978, two women and two Sherpas reach the top, at over 8,000 metres. The first Americans – and the first women, Irene Miller and Vera Karmakova, stand on the summit of Annapurna.

6

Death on the Mountain

Arlene did not hear about the summit success immediately. At the time when Irene and Vera Karmakova were at the top of Annapurna, Arlene was coming down the Dutch Rib alone. As she got to the bottom of the dangerous Rib, she saw Christy Trews, the Base Camp Manager, running towards her. 'Did they reach the summit?' she asked her. Christy smiled and said yes. Arlene was so happy that she sat down in the snow and cried.

That evening Arlene talked to the successful women on the radio. 'How are you feeling?' she asked Irene.

'Getting to Camp 5 and the summit was the hardest thing I've ever done in my life. I'm happy, but now I'm so exhausted . . .' Irene replied.

'What about Piro?' Arlene asked. 'What happened to her?'

Vera Karmakova told her that on the morning of the summit attempt, Piro had discovered that the first finger on her right hand had frozen. If she continued to climb, she could lose the use of her fingers, so she had to go down. Because of this, Irene and Vera Karmakova had sensibly decided to take the Sherpas with them to the summit. More climbers meant that it was safer. If someone was hurt, the others could fetch help.

'Let's go to Kathmandu and have a party!' said one of the Sherpas. He was not the only person who wanted the expedition to get off the mountain as quickly as possible. The weather was getting worse and Arlene hoped that she could persuade Vera Watson and Alison not to try for the summit. The supplies of oxygen were now very small, and none of the Sherpas wanted to go back up the mountain.

'We'll go up to Camp 5 at least, and then we can decide if it's possible,' said Vera.

Arlene agreed, because she knew how hard they had worked on the expedition, and that they both really wanted to reach the summit themselves. She was worried about them, but she knew that they had to try.

Vera Watson and Alison spent that night at Camp 4 with the successful summit team, and went off early next morning towards Camp 5. That evening, Arlene lost radio contact with them. 'Perhaps the radio's not working,' thought Arlene, but the next day there was no sight of them on the mountain.

Irene Miller, who knew what conditions were like at Camp 5 and above, talked about the possibilities. 'They may be resting in their tents for the day, if they're exhausted. That's possible . . . but they can't survive for very long in that cold.' Everyone felt sick with worry.

That night, October 18th, Arlene asked the Sherpas to go up and look for Vera and Alison.

'Do not worry, Bara Memsahib, Alison and Vera are just resting,' a Sherpa told Arlene.

Arlene hoped that he was right, but she spent a sleepless night, and wondered why she had not stopped Alison and Vera.

The next two days seemed endless as the women waited for the two climbers to appear. Many times they thought that they could see a movement high on the mountain, but they were always mistaken.

'Come back down,' said Arlene sadly. 'There's nothing you can do.'

On October 20th, Arlene could wait no longer. She asked the Sherpas to go back up the mountain to look for the women. Some time later she received a radio call: 'We can see the bodies of Alison and Vera between Camp 4 and Camp 5. They have fallen 500 metres down snow and ice. Their bodies are still roped together.'

'Come back down,' said Arlene sadly. 'There's nothing you can do.'

On October 23rd, the women came together at Base Camp and stood around a memorial stone, on which were the names of Vera Watson and Alison Chadwick. These two climbers had stood here two months earlier and had looked up at the summit of Annapurna with so much hope. All the women felt very sad as they looked at the stone and remembered Vera and Alison, but deep inside they knew that their friends had died doing something they really loved.

Now, for the last time, Arlene looked round at this group of friends: at Margi, the young climber who had learnt so much on this expedition; at Annie, still very much in love with Yeshi; at Piro, who had almost climbed to the summit; at Christy, their Base Camp Manager; at Joan, who had almost recovered from her illness; and at Irene, and Vera Karmakova, the successful summit climbers. All of them had worked so hard to make the dream come true. Annapurna had cruelly taken away two very dear friends – but it had given them all so much.

Alone around the World

Dartmouth is a small, busy port on the south coast of England. Every day many ships and small boats enter and leave its harbour. On the morning of 9th September 1977, a very special boat was leaving Dartmouth and hundreds of people, including newspaper and television reporters, had come to watch. The boat was the 53-foot yacht, *Express Crusader*. On it was a 28-year-old woman who was starting an extraordinary journey that would take her 55,000 kilometres around the world. Her name was Naomi James and her plan was to sail single-handed across the world's most dangerous seas. If she succeeded, she would be the first woman to sail alone and non-stop around the world.

1

Beginnings

Naomi Power was born on her parents' farm in Hawkes Bay, New Zealand, in 1949. The farm was in the middle of beautiful, green countryside. Young Naomi spent her childhood playing in the fields around the farm. She had a brother and two older sisters. None of the children had any interest in the sea – their main sporting interest was horse-riding. In fact, Naomi did not even learn to swim until she was twenty-three years old.

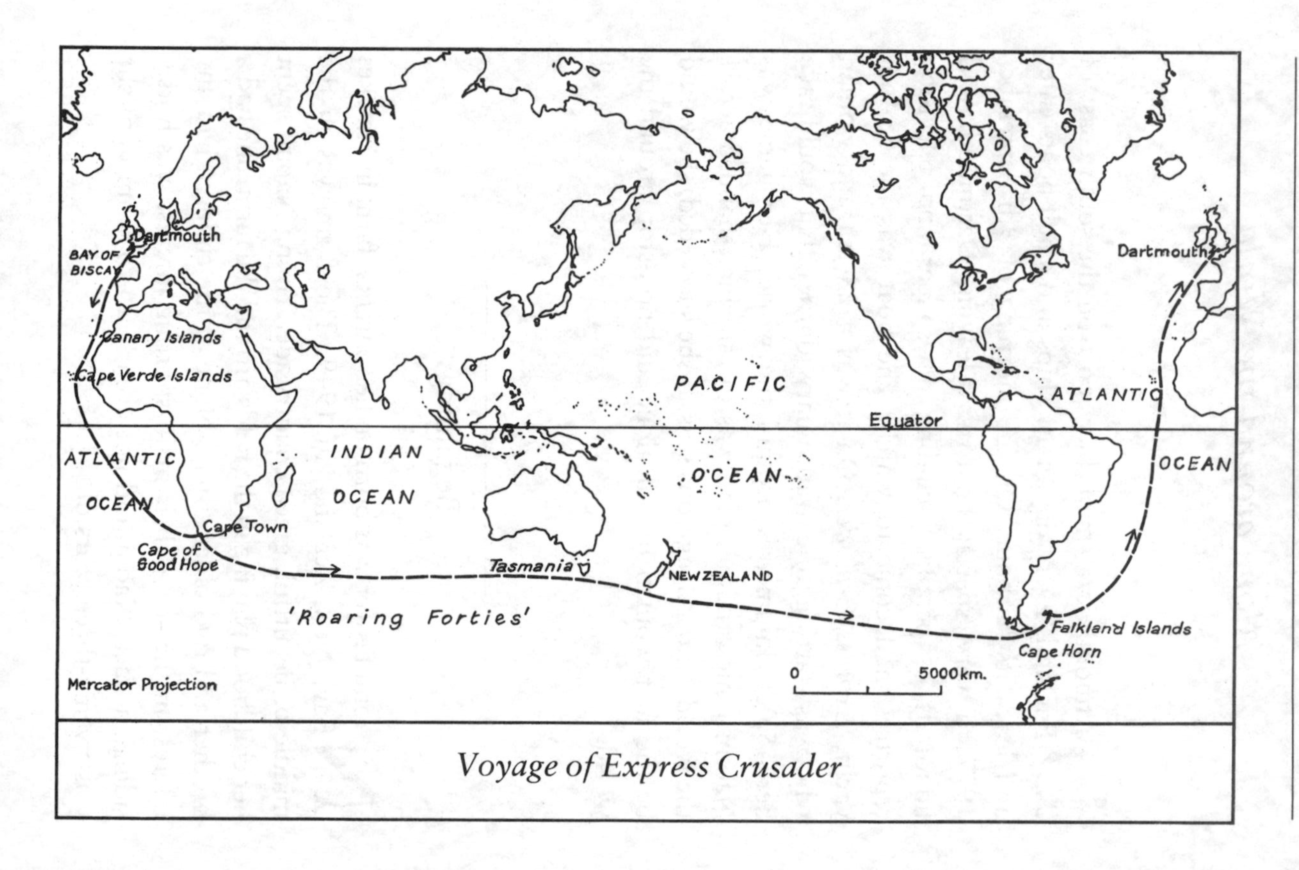

Voyage of Express Crusader

As a child, Naomi spent a lot of time reading. She loved adventure stories about men and women who did exciting, unusual things. She liked to be alone, and often imagined that she was the person who was having these wonderful adventures. However, she was not very successful at school, and she left at the age of sixteen to train as a hairdresser.

'How stupid I was to leave school without taking any exams!' said Naomi to her elder sister, Juliet, some months later. Work at the hairdresser's salon was boring, and the women who worked there were so different from her. So Naomi went to evening classes to study Art, and then German. She decided that she wanted to travel to Europe, but she needed money to do this. So, for the next three years, until she was twenty-one, she saved for her trip.

On 31st December 1970, Naomi and Juliet left New Zealand for Europe. Naomi was very seasick on the voyage to England. She was clearly not a good sailor. The two girls spent ten months in London, where Naomi again worked as a hairdresser. They then moved on to Austria. 'What am I going to do with my life?' was the question Naomi often asked herself during this time. She tried many different jobs, but could not find anything she really liked. She was very shy and did not have much confidence. Because of this, she still preferred to be alone and found it difficult to make friends.

During the next two years, Naomi travelled around a lot in Europe. She was still looking for the adventure and excitement she had read about in those books in New Zealand. Would she ever find something that she really wanted to do, or somewhere she really wanted to be? In the summer of 1973, in Vienna, she bought herself a bicycle and decided to travel alone around Austria. She was now sure of two things: firstly, that she loved travelling, and secondly, that she preferred travelling alone. Very soon, however, Naomi's life was going to change. And it changed in a way that she had never dreamed about back on the family farm in New Zealand.

2

Crazy about Boats

It was August 1975 and Naomi was in France. She began to think seriously about her future. She knew that she liked animals and the open-air life. Why not go to England and try to find work in a zoo?

She sent her bicycle back to Juliet, who was still in Vienna, and went to St Malo in France to catch the boat to England. As she was walking along by the harbour, she stopped to look at the famous yacht *British Steel*. To Naomi's surprise, a young woman suddenly appeared from below deck, and said, 'Would you like a cup of coffee?'

Naomi smiled and accepted the invitation from the friendly stranger. They started talking. The girl was from New Zealand too and she and her husband were having a sailing holiday on *British Steel*.

Naomi learnt that *British Steel* belonged to Chay Blyth, the famous British yachtsman, and that he had sailed it around the world, alone and non-stop. Naomi became very interested and wanted to know more.

'Would you like to come below deck and meet the

captain?' asked the young woman. 'He's been sailing all night and he's just waking up.'

So Naomi followed the girl below deck and there she met Rob James – the man who later became her husband.

At that first meeting, Naomi and Rob talked for hours. They got on very well together. As Naomi listened to Rob's stories of the sea, she became more and more excited. Perhaps this was the kind of adventure she had been looking for. To her surprise, at the end of their talk Rob offered her a job as deckhand and cook on the yacht. Although she knew nothing about boats and could not cook, Naomi accepted immediately. She was always interested in trying something new, and as well as that, she liked Rob very much.

The English Channel is a narrow piece of water between France and England. Although it is only thirty-five kilometres wide, the Channel often has storms and the sea can be very rough. On her first trips across the Channel, Naomi was very seasick and she was afraid that she would never be a sailor. However, little by little things began to get better. Rob was a very good teacher, and Naomi quickly learnt the basics of sailing with his help.

Naomi and Rob soon became very good friends. So Naomi was very unhappy when she learnt that he was going away for six months. He was going to be *British Steel's* captain in the Atlantic Triangle boat race. Rob wanted Naomi to join him in the race, but unfortunately, she did not have enough money for the trip. Instead, she decided to go back to New Zealand for a few months. She had not seen her family now for five years. Leaving Rob was difficult, but she knew that she would soon see him again.

3

I Want to Sail around the World

Back in New Zealand, Naomi was reading a magazine in her parents' living room one day. As she turned the pages, she suddenly saw:

> French woman plans single-handed
> voyage around the world

Naomi was immediately interested, and began to read. The young French woman was planning to sail around the world stopping at many ports on the way. The whole voyage would take three years. Naomi now began to dream – What an adventure that would be! But why not try to do it non-stop?

Express Crusader

No woman had ever done this before. The idea was rather alarming, but, at the same time, very exciting.

Chay Blyth's *The Impossible Voyage* was the first book that Naomi read about single-handed voyages around the world. She read many more: books by famous sailors such as Sir Francis Chichester and Robin Knox-Johnson. The more she read, the more the idea seemed possible. At the end of her stay in New Zealand, she was certain about two things. She wanted to spend the rest of her life with Rob, and she wanted to sail single-handed around the world. She decided to talk to Rob about her plans as soon as she saw him again.

Naomi flew back to England in March 1976, and she and Rob were married at the end of May. However, Naomi was a little worried about telling Rob that she wanted to sail around the world. Perhaps he would think she did not have enough experience, that it was a stupid and dangerous thing to do. In fact, Rob was very enthusiastic about Naomi's plan, though he tried to warn her about the dangers.

'Sailing single-handed is the most dangerous way to sail,' he told her. 'Remember that if you fall off the boat, there's not much chance that you will get on again.'

The idea of falling into the sea and drowning frightened Naomi very much, but she knew that there were ways of preventing this disaster. She could, for example, put ropes over the side of the boat so that she could hold onto them if she fell into the sea. That would give her at least a small chance of surviving.

'The other problem', said Rob, 'is that there are times when you will be very, very tired, and you won't be able to

Naomi James

take a rest, because there's no one else to help. For example, in a long storm you'll need to stay awake all the time.'

A Sailomat would help with this problem. This was a piece of equipment which could steer the boat automatically when Naomi was resting, or doing something else. It was the most important piece of equipment for a single-handed sailor, as it meant that she would not have to spend all her time at the wheel, steering the boat.

When they had discussed the problems and dangers, they began to think about where they could find a boat. They would also need a sponsor.

'You'll need at least £60,000 to buy and refit a boat,' Rob told her. 'Chay Blyth may help. He has a lot of experience in finding sponsors.'

But it was more difficult than they expected. Many people thought that Naomi was crazy to try to sail alone in the world's most difficult seas. She did not have enough experience. However, Naomi did not lose hope. She knew that she had to be confident herself if she wanted other people to have confidence in her.

Then, one evening, her luck changed. She was at Chay's house for dinner when one of the guests began to talk about sponsorship. 'It would be much easier to get a sponsor if you took a boat like *The Spirit of Cutty Sark* (which belonged to Chay). Then you would only need about £10,000 for the refit. You'd have to change the boat for single-handed sailing.'

Then a man named Quentin Wallop, who owned a yacht himself, said: 'OK, I'll sponsor you for £10,000.'

Naomi was too surprised to speak, but she was much more surprised when Chay suddenly looked up and said: 'If you put in the money, Quentin, I'll let Naomi use *The Spirit of Cutty Sark*.'

Naomi could not sleep that night. She lay awake thinking about her chance to be the first woman to sail single-handed and non-stop around the world. And in such a wonderful yacht! The most difficult part of the voyage would be Cape Horn. She knew that she had to sail round it no later than March in order to be sure of good weather. So she would have to leave England in early September. She had about a month to prepare the boat – and herself.

Saying goodbye to Rob was the worst part. He left two weeks before Naomi because he was sailing in a yacht race. Although they were prepared for it, both of them had tears in their eyes when the moment came to say goodbye. They had been together for only a short time. Naomi also knew that she might never see him again. She was going on an extremely dangerous voyage and she might never return. 'I must stop thinking about that,' she told herself. 'I have to think about the job ahead.'

From now on, Naomi thought only about her preparations for the voyage. She would have to work day and night if she wanted to be ready. All the equipment and sails on the boat had to be checked, and repaired if necessary. As well as the Sailomat, she would need a radio telephone and navigation equipment. Naomi smiled to herself when she thought about navigating. Rob had been a good teacher, but she was still not a very good navigator. She hoped to learn more about it on the voyage.

Then there was the food. Maureen Blyth, Chay's wife, helped Naomi to get it all ready. They had to prepare each tin of food for the voyage. They had to take off the labels and write the names of the food on the tins in a special pen. This was because the tins could easily become wet during the voyage. And if the labels came off, Naomi would not know what was inside the tins. Maureen spent many hours at this job. Juliet, Naomi's sister, also helped by carefully packing Naomi's clothes in plastic bags. Everything on the boat had to be waterproof.

In the middle of all this preparation, Naomi received some very good news. A newspaper called the *Daily Express* agreed to give some money to Naomi's round-the-world voyage. The editor of the newspaper wanted Naomi to write some stories about her voyage. He also wanted the yacht to have a different name – *Express Crusader*. Naomi needed the money desperately, as she was beginning to realize what an expensive adventure it was.

4

From Dartmouth to the Equator

'It's hopeless! You can't start tomorrow – the boat's just not ready.' This was Andrew, one of Naomi's helpers. It was the 2nd September 1977, and Naomi had gone to visit the boat for a last check before the voyage. Her heart sank. Would the boat ever be ready? It seemed that every time things were almost finished, something went wrong at the last moment. And there were so many things that could go wrong. All the different sails, the engine, the radio, the Sailomat, which Naomi had to order from Sweden . . . the list was endless.

In the end, it was 9th September before Naomi and the boat were ready to go. As she sailed out of Dartmouth, surrounded by family and friends in other boats, she knew that from now on she would be completely alone. Well, almost completely alone . . . In single-handed sailing no other person was allowed to go onto the boat after the voyage had started. Luckily this rule did not include animals. One of Naomi's friends had given her a young cat to take on the boat. Naomi named the small black kitten 'Boris', and during the difficult months ahead, he became her greatest friend.

As she sailed towards the Channel Islands, Naomi felt happy and confident. At last she was on her way. For the moment she only had to worry about seasickness (both she and Boris were seasick), but very soon she would have more dangerous problems – ships. This sea route was very busy and a big ship could very easily run into a small yacht like *Express Crusader*. The night was the most dangerous time. Naomi knew that it would only take twenty minutes for a ship to come over the horizon and hit her. For the first seven nights, her alarm clock rang every twenty minutes to wake her up. After that week she was completely exhausted, but alive!

During the voyage, Naomi kept a log book (a ship's 'diary') every day. It kept her busy and stopped her from feeling lonely. On 15th September *Express Crusader* was sailing in the Bay of Biscay. Naomi wrote in her log book:

> Last night and today have been terrible – I've only been sailing for six days and everything's going wrong!

At two o'clock in the morning Naomi had been woken by the noise of a very strong wind. She left her warm bed and ran up on deck. There she found that part of the rudder on the Sailomat was broken. Naomi immediately tried to repair it, but suddenly the rudder slipped out of her hands and fell into the icy cold sea. She could not believe her eyes as she watched it disappear. Fortunately, she had another rudder, but it took her hours to fix it on. And in the middle of the night!

By Day 12, however, Naomi was on course for the Canary Islands. The weather was good and the sea calm. At the Canaries, a boat came out to meet her with some supplies and another rudder for the Sailomat. She needed an extra one in case she had another disaster.

More extracts from the log book:

Day 18
Cape Town here I come. I can still see one of the Canary Islands in the distance. The wind is blowing between 20 and 30 knots. I feel much happier now that I have an extra rudder . . .

Day 20
The weather is very difficult. Sometimes there's no wind at all, other times it's 30 knots. No clouds. Maybe I can sleep tonight if the wind drops. I've just eaten potatoes, peas and eggs. Rob would be pleased! He advised me to eat regularly and well. Doing everything yourself is so tiring . . .

Day 23 (1st October)
I sailed about 240 kilometres yesterday and 190 today. There's no wind again and the sails hang loose over the boat . . .

Day 26
I passed the Cape Verde Islands today. Boris has found a new game – to jump up at one of sails and try to catch it. Last night he had a fight with a flying fish which landed on deck. Neither Boris nor I like this hot weather . . .

Day 28
I've got sunstroke. I spent too long in the hot sun yesterday when I was on deck repairing the Sailomat. Today I have to stay below, lying on my bed and reading . . .

'Sometimes there's no wind at all, other times it's 30 knots.'

Day 30
The radio has stopped working. I've looked at it, but have no idea what the problem is. I feel very bad, mainly because I know that Rob is waiting for my call . . .

Day 32
The radio is still not working. It's 8,000 kilometres to Cape Town. I'm so worried that I may have to stop there so that I can get the radio repaired. For the first time I'm feeling very miserable . . .

Day 34
In a strange way it's nice not having a radio. I've got used to it . . . that feeling of being completely alone. But I'm happy to have little Boris . . .

Day 38
At last I've crossed the Equator! I opened a packet from Juliet which she gave me to open on this day – a new book of stories. I also cooked myself a celebration dinner: vegetable soup, meat, potatoes, onions and peas – and a bottle of champagne!

5

Cape Town

As *Express Crusader* went south, Naomi wondered about the next part of the journey. What would the weather be like round the Cape of Good Hope and in the 'Roaring Forties'? These were the most difficult seas of the journey. She knew that she should expect strong winds and storms. She began to prepare herself by reading books on the subject.

What should the single-handed sailor do in a bad storm? One of the books explained two things she could do. First, she could 'lie a-hull'. This meant taking down the sails, tying up the wheel and going below deck with the cabin door shut. Secondly, she could 'stream warps'. This meant putting very heavy ropes over the stern, or back, of the boat to make it travel slowly, and stop it from leaving its course. Naomi preferred to 'stream warps'. She thought that *Express Crusader* could capsize if she tried to 'lie a-hull'. Capsizing, or turning over completely, was a real possibility in a very bad storm.

It was Day 50. Naomi was 27° south and 23° west. She was still 3,500 kilometres from Cape Town, but she hoped to be there in three weeks. She still had no radio and so was unable to make contact with the rest of the world. She worried about Rob, and her family in New Zealand. They did not know whether she was alive or dead.

The radio was a problem, but not really a disaster. Worse things followed . . .

The next day, Boris was playing on the deck as usual, when he fell into the sea. Naomi had turned away from him for a moment, and he had fallen into the water. She looked for him for two hours, watching the water, hoping that his little face would appear. But it did not. 'Boris has gone,' Naomi wrote sadly in her log book. She thought about his little games and knew that she would miss him terribly. He had been her only friend on this long voyage. The accident also made her realize that if she fell from the boat, she would also drown. That was a very frightening idea.

Then on Day 56, Naomi realized that she had been making a silly mistake in her navigation. 'Rob would not think much of this,' she told herself, and she worked very hard for the next few days to understand the problem and find the right answer. Working hard helped her to forget her sadness at losing Boris.

On 3rd November at six o'clock in the morning came the storm she had expected for so long. She was woken by the awful noise of the wind. Naomi measured the wind at 30 to 40 knots. During the next twenty-four hours it went up to 60 knots. She waited all day for the wind to drop, hoping that the Sailomat would keep *Crusader* on course. Her worst fear was that the boat would capsize, because then she could lose the mast. She slept for only one and a half hours that night. But at two o'clock the next afternoon the wind began to drop, and the worst of the storm was over.

Some days later, Naomi discovered that the Sailomat was again very badly damaged, probably because of the storm. This time she realized sadly that she would have to stop in Cape Town for repairs, not only to the Sailomat, but also to the radio. Her chance of sailing around the world non-stop had disappeared. 'I feel so disappointed,' she wrote, 'but I know I am doing the right thing. The success of the voyage depends on it.'

Naomi stayed in Cape Town for three days. A local yachtsman, Jerry Whitehead, offered to repair the Sailomat and promised that it would be ready in two days. The radio too could be repaired quite quickly. Everyone there was so kind, and they helped Naomi to contact Rob and her worried parents. The first night, Naomi had a hot bath and a wonderful dinner. As she went to sleep, she asked herself why she was doing this crazy thing. She could be at home having hot baths and eating good food every night. She did not know the answer. But she did know that she wanted to get back to her boat and to continue her voyage as soon as she could.

6

Around Cape Horn

Naomi was happy to be back at sea after only three days in Cape Town. Now she had to get to Cape Horn before the really bad weather started. She knew that there would be danger from storms and icebergs. She had stopped at a port, so it was no longer a non-stop voyage, but that did not matter. The important thing was to finish what she had started, to prove to herself that she could do it.

Day 79 (26th November)
Spoke to Rob! I'm rather frightened about going around Cape Horn, but he made me feel better. He advised me not to go too far south around the Horn as it's too cold and there are too many icebergs. We talked for twenty-seven minutes . . .

By mid-December, Naomi had travelled 17,000 kilometres, an average of 165 kilometres a day. On 20th December, the weather suddenly became worse. There was a strong wind and the waves were very high. All night Naomi lay on her bed wearing her oilskins, waiting. At midday the next day, a very big wave broke over the side of the boat and went into the map room. The boat was pushed over on its side. Naomi's heart started beating very fast. Would *Crusader* get back up? Luckily, after a few seconds, which seemed to Naomi like an hour, the boat came back up. This was the first time that *Crusader* had been knocked down, but it would not be the last.

As December 25th came nearer, Naomi began to think about Christmas. How would she feel about spending this special time in the middle of the ocean, away from her family and friends?

She wrote in a story for the *Daily Express:*

> On 23rd December, two days before Christmas Day, I began to celebrate already because I was exactly halfway around the world. I opened a bottle of wine and ate some chocolate. Perhaps the best thing is just to eat and drink, to think of my family and friends, and then I won't feel too lonely . . .

During January, Naomi sailed around the southern coast of Tasmania, Australia. On 15th January (Day 129), a boat came out to meet her, carrying equipment and fresh food. Bern Cuthbertson, the captain of that boat, brought her fruit, bread, butter, and some letters from her family – and from Rob. For Naomi it was like Christmas again. She sent a telegram to her family in New Zealand. She told them that she would contact them by radio as she got nearer to their home. It would be so wonderful to hear their voices after so long.

The next few days were a good time for Naomi. She read and reread her letters from Rob. The weather was not quite so cold now, and Naomi was able to spend more time on deck. It also gave her more time to think about her life. She kept asking herself the question: 'Why am I doing this? Why am I putting my life in danger?' Although she had lost her chance to be the first woman to sail around the world non-stop, she still wanted to break a record. She wanted to beat the time set by Sir Francis Chichester in his yacht, Gipsy Moth. So she would have to be in England before 10th June. This meant reaching Cape Horn by 14th March. It seemed possible as *Express Crusader* was sailing very well. But,

'Why am I doing this? Why am I putting my life in danger?'

unfortunately for Naomi, her good luck did not continue. On 27th February, in the worst storm of the voyage, the boat capsized.

Naomi described the experience in her log book:

> The waves were enormous – over 10 metres high, and *Crusader* was thrown around like a child's toy. I had no control at all. The boat capsized at 5 a.m., but came back up again after a long pause. A lot of water came into the cabin, and equipment on deck was broken by the violence of the waves. I pumped the water out quickly, frightened that the boat was sinking. Then I tied myself to the wheel and steered for the next nine hours. After a while in that terrible storm, I stopped feeling afraid, and just felt nothing at all. When the wind finally dropped, I went below deck to look at the damage. A lot of things were wet, broken or lost, but the boat was still in one piece. I fell asleep, exhausted.

Naomi now had to make a very difficult decision. Would she go back to New Zealand to repair the damage? Or would she continue? She knew now just how dangerous her voyage was. There could be more storms like that one. However, the only reason for going back was fear. If she could control her fear, and just hope for good luck . . . In the end, she knew that she had to go on. She had to succeed.

Naomi pushed *Crusader* on, further and further south, towards Cape Horn, the tip of South America. Fortunately, there were no more bad storms and finally, on 20th March, Naomi sailed round the famous Cape Horn. 'I've done it!' she wrote. 'Last night I slept for four hours, my longest sleep for six months.' She had been through the bad times and she had survived. The most difficult part of the voyage was finished. Surely there could only be better times ahead.

A few days after going round the Horn, in freezing weather, Naomi stopped for three days in the Falkland Islands. There, she had the mast repaired. The Islanders were friendly and helpful, but the place was wild and cold. She looked forward to the warm weather of the Equator.

7

Homewards

From now on, Naomi sailed an average of 200 kilometres a day for most of the time. She stayed one day ahead of Sir Francis Chichester's time, and hoped to beat his record. Some days there was not enough wind. Other days there were sudden storms. These changes in the weather annoyed Naomi but still the kilometres rushed by. Her plan was to arrive in Dartmouth on 8th June. Juliet and her husband, Heini, would be there to welcome Naomi back. Her mother and father would also be in Dartmouth as they had travelled to England to see her return. An even better surprise followed.

On 2nd May (Day 237) Naomi wrote in her log book:

> Still 2,000 kilometres to go to Dartmouth but *Crusader* is sailing beautifully. Wonderful news today – Rob and I will meet near the Azores. Although he can't come on board, we'll be able to talk to each other face to face.

The meeting with Rob on 24th May went as well as Naomi had hoped, and, although they had to stay on separate boats, they were able to talk about their hopes and feelings and dreams. Four days later, Naomi wrote in her log book:

> 250 kilometres today! One of my best days' sailing and now I'm only about 1,000 kilometres from Dartmouth. Ships are the biggest problem, so I've started sleeping only half an hour at a time again. I was almost hit last night – really frightening!

Crusader continued to sail extremely well, and on 2nd June, Naomi was only 75 kilometres away from Dartmouth. Unless there was some terrible disaster, she was going to beat Chichester's time easily. But she knew that she could not

Welcome back to Dartmouth
(Rob is standing next to Naomi)

arrive before the agreed day and time: 9.30 on the morning of June 8th. Hundreds of people would be there on that day, waiting to welcome her back from her long voyage. Anyway, now that she was almost there, Naomi realized that she was no longer in a hurry. She wanted to enjoy her last few days of being alone. She spent these days cleaning the boat so that *Express Crusader* would look beautiful for her entry into Dartmouth harbour.

As she sailed into Dartmouth on the morning of 8th June 1978, Naomi was certainly not alone. She was surrounded by boats, large and small. She could see reporters and TV cameras. Her mother and father were there, and Juliet and Heini . . . and of course Rob. Everyone was looking at her, cheering, welcoming her back from her voyage. As she greeted them, she realized that she could never be really alone again. She also realized that, although she was happy to be back, she was going to miss that wonderful feeling of freedom, of being alone with the sea.

GLOSSARY

Aborigine a black person from Australia
advertisement a notice (e.g. in a newspaper) telling people about jobs, things to sell, etc.
altitude the height of something, especially above sea level
avalanche a sudden fall of rocks or snow down the side of a mountain
base *(n)* the lowest part of something; **base camp** the main camp (at the bottom of the mountain)
blind not able to see
break a record to do better (e.g. in sport) than anyone has ever done before
bush wild country (especially in Australia)
camel a big animal with one or two humps on its back, usually found in the desert (a bull camel is a male camel)
camp *(v)* to put up tents; *(n)* a place where people live for a time, usually in tents
capsize (of a boat) to turn over in the sea
celebrate to do something to show that a day or event is special
cheer *(v)* to shout to show that you are pleased with someone
compass an instrument used for showing direction (e.g. north, south, east, west)
crevasse a crack or hole in a glacier
deck the floor of a ship or boat
deckhand a sailor who works on a boat or ship
desert a very dry, sandy piece of country e.g. the Sahara Desert
equipment special things you need to do a job
establish (of a camp) to make a camp, put up tents, etc.
expedition a journey to do something special or to find out about something

glacier a river of ice
harbour a place on a coast where ships can stop safely
horizon the line at which land (or sea) and sky seem to meet
huge very big
iceberg a very large piece of ice which floats in the sea
injection putting medicine through the skin into the body with a needle
knot a unit of speed used by ships; one nautical mile per hour (a nautical, or sea, mile is about 1,852 metres)
load *(n)* something that you carry
mast a tall, straight piece of wood or metal that stands on a boat to hold the sails
member someone who belongs to a group or team
memorial something (e.g. a building) to remind people of someone or something
mentally of the mind
monsoon very heavy rain, usually in Asia
muzzle *(n)* something that is put over an animal's mouth so that it cannot eat or bite
navigate to use a map to find which way a ship should go
oilskins clothes made of waterproof material, often worn by sailors
on course going in the right direction
physically of the body
poison something that can kill you or make you very ill if you eat it
port a town or city with a harbour
porter a person (in hotels, stations, airports, etc.) who carries bags
pump *(v)* to use a machine that moves water or air into or out of something

rabbit a small animal, with long ears, that lives in holes under the ground
refit to make a boat or ship ready to go to sea
rifle a long gun which you hold against your shoulder when you fire it
rope very thick, strong string
rudder a flat piece of wood at the back of a boat or ship that you move to make the boat go left or right
saddle a seat for a rider on a horse's or camel's back
sponsor *(n)* a person or a company that gives money, equipment, help, etc. for special activities or sporting events
sponsor *(v)* to act as a sponsor for somebody or something
steer to turn a wheel or handle to guide a boat, car, bike, etc.
summit the top of a mountain
sunstroke an illness caused by too much sun on the head
supplies equipment, food, etc. that people need
swing *(v)* to move backwards and forwards through the air
tent a house made of cloth over poles
tracks rough marks on the ground that people, animals, cars, etc. make as they go along
treat to behave in a certain way (e.g. well, badly) towards someone or something
waterproof which keeps out water, e.g. a raincoat is waterproof
yacht a kind of boat which usually has sails
yard a piece of hard ground, usually next to a building

ACTIVITIES

Before Reading

1 **Read the introduction on the first page of the book, and the back cover. Which journey does each sentence describe? Circle R (for Robyn's), A (for Arlene's), or N (for Naomi's).**

1 She was alone on a boat for more than eight months. R/A/N
2 She used animals to help her make her journey. R/A/N
3 Her journey took her to a cold and dangerous place. R/A/N
4 Two women died on her journey. R/A/N
5 Her journey began and ended in the same place. R/A/N
6 Her journey took her to a hot and empty place. R/A/N

2 **What kind of person do you need to be for adventures like these? Put this list in order of importance (with number 1 for the most important).**

You need to be . . .

1 brave.
2 physically strong.
3 mentally strong.
4 able to keep going when you are exhausted.
5 able to laugh when times are difficult.
6 good at planning and thinking ahead.
7 able to recognize dangerous situations and avoid them.
8 someone who never takes 'no' for an answer.

ACTIVITIES

While Reading

Across the Australian Desert

Read the story. Are these sentences true (T) or false (F)? Rewrite the false ones with the correct information.

1 When Robyn arrived in Alice Springs, she had a lot of money and had worked with camels before.
2 Kurt made Robyn work hard and treated the camels badly.
3 Kurt made Robyn leave his farm because he didn't like her.
4 Robyn had to sell Alcoota Kate because she was dangerous.
5 Robyn borrowed money to buy Bub and Dookie.
6 Ayers Rock is a place that is special to the Aborigines.
7 Old Mr Eddie couldn't walk thirty-two kilometres a day.
8 In the desert it was hot in the daytime, and also hot at night.
9 Diggity died from eating poison that was meant for dingos.
10 After Diggity died, Robyn did not want to carry on.
11 It was the first time any of the camels had seen the sea.

Different people said these things to Robyn before or during her journey. Who or what were they talking about?

1 'Don't worry, love. It won't be long now.'
2 'Shoot first, and ask questions later!'
3 'Women aren't allowed to go to some of these places.'
4 'The land can own *them*, but they can't own the land.'
5 'Little bit long way, maybe two sleeps.'

Climbing Annapurna

Read the story, and complete this text with the best words.

_____ to the Himalayas need careful planning. Only a few climbers can hope to reach the _____, and everybody has to work as a _____, carrying equipment up to the _____. Some climbers use Sherpas, who make excellent _____ and who can carry very heavy _____.

At high _____ people often have headaches and sleep badly because there is not much _____ in the air. Weather _____ can change very quickly, and there is also great danger from _____, which are impossible to avoid.

Choose the best question-word for these questions, and then answer them.

How / Why / What / Who

1 . . . did the women want to climb Annapurna?
2 . . . many people die while climbing in the Himalayas?
3 . . . would happen if the climbers didn't have enough different kinds of food?
4 . . . did the team wait until the middle of September before going above Camp 2?
5 . . . was 'The Dutch Rib'?
6 . . . had Yeshi become a cook?
7 . . . many teams were going to try for the summit?
8 . . . were the first women to reach the top of Annapurna?
9 . . . did Piro decide not to climb to the summit?
10 . . . happened to Alison Chadwick and Vera Watson?

Alone around the World

Read the story, and then complete these sentences with the names of people, places, or boats.

1 Naomi grew up on a farm in the country of _____ _____.
2 After a few years travelling around _____, Naomi decided to go to _____ to find work in a zoo.
3 She was about to catch a boat at _____ _____, when she met _____ _____, the captain of *British Steel*.
4 A famous British yachtsman, _____ _____, offered her his boat for the voyage.
5 Naomi set off in his yacht, with its new name of _____ _____, in September 1977.
6 After two weeks, she reached the _____ _____ and a boat brought her supplies.
7 On day 38 Naomi crossed the _____ and had a celebration dinner and a bottle of champagne.
8 When Naomi was 3,500 kilometres from _____ _____, Boris fell into the sea and was lost.
9 In January, she passed the coast of _____.
10 She hoped to break the record set by _____ _____ _____.
11 Three weeks before she reached _____ _____, at the tip of _____ _____, Naomi's boat capsized.
12 She spent three days in the _____ _____ while her mast was repaired.
13 On 24th May she met _____ near the _____.
14 When she sailed into _____ on 8th June 1978, Naomi became the first woman to sail alone around the world.

ACTIVITIES

After Reading

1 **Perhaps this is what Robyn, Arlene, and Naomi were thinking at different moments in their journeys. Which thoughts belong to which person (each has two), and what had just happened?**

1 'I just can't believe he's gone. He was always climbing about everywhere and playing games. I've looked and looked for him, but it's hopeless. I'm going to miss him terribly. And it's frightening to think that the same thing could happen to me . . .'

2 'That lazy, mean man! After all those months of hard work, seven days a week – and he just tells me to go! What am I going to do? It's the end of my dream. I'll have to go back to Adelaide . . .'

3 'What was that? Something woke me – oh God, I can hear it now. It's a really frightening sound, and you can hear it even above the terrible noise of this wind. It was a crazy idea to come here. We could all be killed . . .'

4 'She's so thin. Her poor baby doesn't understand why I want to keep him away from his mother, but I don't want him to get sick too. I just hope the medicine will keep her alive until we get to the farm. It would be so sad if we couldn't all finish the journey together . . .'

5 'Oh, why has this happened? Everybody knew the rules, and agreed to them. But I can't tell her to fall out of love! I just hope it doesn't make problems in the team . . .'

6 'It's freezing, but I'm feeling great after four hours' sleep. The hardest part of the voyage is over, and I still have a chance to break the record. Thank goodness it's going to get warmer soon . . .'

2 **Here is a newspaper report about Robyn Davidson's journey. Find the best endings to complete the sentences, and join them with these linking words.**

after / although / as / in order to / that / which

1 _____ walking 2,800 kilometres across the Australian desert,
2 Crowds of people came to watch
3 Robyn spent eighteen months in Alice Springs preparing for the journey,
4 _____ she travelled with a guide for part of the journey,
5 Robyn feels proud and happy
6 She plans to stay by the sea for a while,

7 she crossed the Gibson Desert alone.
8 Robyn Davidson arrived today at Hamelin Pool.
9 _____ rest and make plans for the future.
10 _____ this brave young woman brought her four camels onto the beach.
11 _____ her four camels all survived the journey.
12 _____ took her six months to complete.

3 **Here is a newspaper report about Arlene Blum's journey, but it is full of mistakes. Can you find and correct them?**

CLIMBER ARLENE BLUM returned today from India, where she led an expedition to climb Annapurna, the highest mountain in the world. Her group of eight women were aged between thirty and sixty, and none of them were used to high-altitude mountaineering. They began climbing the easiest part of the mountain after the monsoon rains began, and established Camp 5, their lowest camp, at 7,500 metres. On October 15th three British women and one Sherpa reached the summit, which is over 9,000 metres high. Sadly, two other climbers died in an accident while trying to reach the summit. A memorial stone with their names has been put up at Camp 5.

4 **Now use these notes to write a similar newspaper report about Naomi James's voyage.**

- today / Naomi James / first woman / alone / world / when / sailed / Dartmouth / *Express Crusader*
- end / 55,000-kilometre voyage / lasted / nine months / took her east / Cape of Good Hope / Australia / New Zealand / Cape Horn
- worst moment / February / boat / capsized / equipment broken / able / sleep / an hour or two / decided / go on
- met / Dartmouth / sister / husband / seen / month before / Azores / spoken / radio telephone / left / last September
- *Express Crusader* / surrounded / boats / harbour / 9.30 / hundreds / people / reporters / waiting / welcome / home

5 Which stories could these words be used in? Put each word under one of these headings.

DESERT	MOUNTAIN	SEA	TWO OR THREE STORIES

altitude	deck	leader	porter	steer
avalanche	equipment	load	radio	summit
bush	expedition	log book	repair	supplies
camp	glacier	map	rifle	tent
camel	guide	mast	rope	wave
capsize	harbour	monsoon	rudder	wheel
compass	horizon	navigate	saddle	yacht
crevasse	iceberg	oxygen	Sherpa	

6 Which of the journeys in this book would *you* like to make? Choose one of them, and then make lists of these things.

- four things that you must take with you
- four things that you will miss while you are travelling
- four things that you will be happy to get away from

7 Do you agree (A) or disagree (D) with these ideas? Why, or why not?

1 People will always want to do difficult and dangerous things, and there is no reason why they shouldn't do them.
2 Women who have young children shouldn't go on dangerous adventures like these.
3 Only men should go on dangerous expeditions.
4 Expeditions like these are very expensive, and it would be better to spend the money on something else.

ABOUT THE AUTHORS

SUE LEATHER

Sue Leather has been involved in English Language Teaching since 1989 as a teacher, teacher trainer, manager, and materials writer. She now works freelance from Cambridge, England, but travels all over the world training teachers and managers. She loves reading adventure stories and sometimes going on adventures. She doesn't sail across oceans or cross deserts with camels, but she loves mountain-walking, and her dream is to go to the Himalayas one day, like the women in the *Mountain* story. She once took a group of students up a mountain called Helvellyn in the Lake District in northern England. However, Helvellyn is only 951 metres high.

ROBYN DAVIDSON

Robyn Davidson was born on a cattle station in Queensland, Australia, in 1950, and attended the University of Queensland. When she set out for Alice Springs, she had 'never changed a light-bulb, sewn a dress, mended a sock, changed a tyre, or used a screwdriver', but her dream of training camels and crossing the great desert of Australia with them was to come true. Her journey across the Australian desert was the subject of her first book, *Tracks*, which was published in 1981 and which won the Thomas Cook Travel Book Award. She has since written other books, including a novel, *Ancestors* (1989). In 1992 she spent a year with the Rabari people in Rajasthan, northwest India, and her book *Desert Places* (1996) describes her experiences there.

ARLENE BLUM

Arlene Blum was born in 1945. She has made more than 300 successful ascents, including climbs of Mount Everest, Mount McKinley, and Annapurna, and took part in a 3,200-kilometre trek across Bhutan, Nepal and India. She is also trained in biophysical chemistry and has taught at Stanford University and the University of California (Berkeley) in the United States.

Arlene Blum now uses her experience as a mountaineer and a leader in conducting leadership workshops, teaching people how to make it to the top in their own lives just as she has done on so many mountains. Her book *Annapurna: A Woman's Place* was reissued in 1998 to mark the 20th anniversary of the ascent of Annapurna by her team.

NAOMI JAMES

Naomi James was born in New Zealand in 1949. Just two years after her first experience of sailing, she set out on 9th September 1977 to sail single-handed around the world. When she returned to Britain on 8th June 1978, she became the first woman to achieve this, and she also broke the record for sailing around the world set by Sir Francis Chichester. She was made a Dame Commander of the Order of the British Empire in 1979.

Naomi James's book *At One With the Sea* describes her solo voyage. Her next book, *At Sea on Land*, was about her participation in a single-handed race across the Atlantic. In 1995 she produced a video called *Great Journeys: Across the South Pacific*. She now lives in Gloucestershire, England.

ABOUT BOOKWORMS

OXFORD BOOKWORMS LIBRARY

Classics • True Stories • Fantasy & Horror • Human Interest
Crime & Mystery • Thriller & Adventure

The OXFORD BOOKWORMS LIBRARY offers a wide range of original and adapted stories, both classic and modern, which take learners from elementary to advanced level through six carefully graded language stages:

Stage 1 (400 headwords)
Stage 2 (700 headwords)
Stage 3 (1000 headwords)
Stage 4 (1400 headwords)
Stage 5 (1800 headwords)
Stage 6 (2500 headwords)

More than fifty titles are also available on cassette, and there are many titles at Stages 1 to 4 which are specially recommended for younger learners. In addition to the introductions and activities in each Bookworm, resource material includes photocopiable test worksheets and Teacher's Handbooks, which contain advice on running a class library and using cassettes, and the answers for the activities in the books.

Several other series are linked to the OXFORD BOOKWORMS LIBRARY. They range from highly illustrated readers for young learners, to playscripts, non-fiction readers, and unsimplified texts for advanced learners.

Oxford Bookworms Starters
Oxford Bookworms Playscripts
Oxford Bookworms Factfiles
Oxford Bookworms Collection

Details of these series and a full list of all titles in the OXFORD BOOKWORMS LIBRARY can be found in the *Oxford English* catalogues. A selection of titles from the OXFORD BOOKWORMS LIBRARY can be found on the next pages.

BOOKWORMS • HUMAN INTEREST • STAGE 4

Three Men in a Boat

JEROME K. JEROME

Retold by Diane Mowat

'I like work. I find it interesting . . . I can sit and look at it for hours.'

With ideas like this, perhaps it is not a good idea to spend a holiday taking a boat trip up the River Thames. But this is what the three friends decide to do. It is the sort of holiday that is fun to remember afterwards, but not so much fun to wake up to early on a cold, wet morning.

This famous book has made people laugh all over the world for a hundred years . . . and they are still laughing.

BOOKWORMS • THRILLER & ADVENTURE • STAGE 4

The Moonspinners

MARY STEWART

Retold by Diane Mowat

When Nicola arrives in Crete a day early, she gets more than just an extra day of holiday. She comes to a village where no one can be trusted, and she becomes involved in a murder mystery that puts her own life in danger.

This story is set in a small village in the mountains of Crete. This is an island where people have strong feelings, where arguments begin suddenly, and end quickly. And Nicola has arrived in the middle of an argument that could end very quickly – with a gun.

BOOKWORMS • FANTASY & HORROR • STAGE 4

The Songs of Distant Earth and Other Stories

ARTHUR C. CLARKE

Retold by Jennifer Bassett

'High above them, Lora and Clyde heard a sound their world had not heard for centuries – the thin scream of a starship coming in from outer space, leaving a long white tail like smoke across the clear blue sky. They looked at each other in wonder. After three hundred years of silence, Earth had reached out once more to touch Thalassa . . .'

And with the starship comes knowledge, and love, and pain.

In these five science-fiction stories Arthur C. Clarke takes us travelling through the universe into the unknown but always possible future.

BOOKWORMS • CLASSICS • STAGE 4

Gulliver's Travels

JONATHAN SWIFT

Retold by Clare West

'Soon I felt something alive moving along my leg and up my body to my face, and when I looked down, I saw a very small human being, only fifteen centimetres tall . . . I was so surprised that I gave a great shout.'

But that is only the first of many surprises which Gulliver has on his travels. He visits a land of giants and a flying island, meets ghosts from the past and horses which talk . . .

BOOKWORMS • THRILLER & ADVENTURE • STAGE 4

We Didn't Mean to Go to Sea

ARTHUR RANSOME

Retold by Ralph Mowat

The four Walker children never meant to go to sea. They had promised their mother they would stay safely in the harbour, and would be home on Friday in time for tea.

But there they are in someone else's boat, drifting out to sea in a thick fog. When the fog lifts, they can turn round and sail back to the harbour. But then comes the wind and the storm, driving them out even further across the cold North Sea . . .

BOOKWORMS • HUMAN INTEREST • STAGE 5

Heat and Dust

RUTH PRAWER JHABVALA

Retold by Clare West

Heat and dust – these simple, terrible words describe the Indian summer. Year after year, endlessly, it is the same. And everyone who experiences this heat and dust is changed for ever.

We often say, in these modern times, that sexual relationships have changed, for better or for worse. But in this book we see that things have not changed. Whether we look back sixty years, or a hundred and sixty, we see that it is not things that change, but people. And, in the heat and dust of an Indian summer, even people are not very different after all.